Volume I

CONTEN

GW00367051

Copyright © 1999 Walton Manufacturing Ltd.
3-5 North Frederick Street, Dublin 1, Ireland

Produced by Pat Conway • Photos: The Irish Historical Picture Company
Design by Temple of Design • Printed in Ireland by Betaprint Ltd.

Order No. WM1319
ISBN No. 1 85720 092 6

Exclusive Distributors:
Walton Manufacturing Co. Ltd., Unit 6A, Rosemount Park Drive, Rosemount Business Park, Ballycoolin Road, Blanchardstown, Dublin 15, Ireland
Walton Music Inc., P.O. Box 874, New York, NY 10009, U.S.A.

3 5 7 9 0 8 6 4 2

The Rare Ould Times

Words & Music by Pete St. John

Copyright Pete St. John (MCPS)

My name it is Sean Dempsey, as Dublin as can be
Born hard and late in Pimlico, in a house that ceased to be.
By trade I was a cooper, lost out to redundancy,
Like my house that fell to progress, my trade's a memory.

And I courted Peggy Dignan, as pretty as you please,
A rogue and a Child of Mary, from the rebel Liberties.
I lost her to a student chap, with skin as black as coal,
When he took her off to Birmingham, she took away my soul.
Chorus:– (repeat after last two verses)

The years have made me bitter, the gargle dims my brain,
'Cause Dublin keeps on changing, and nothing seems the same.
The Pillar and the Met. have gone, the Royal long since pulled down,
As the great unyielding concrete makes a city of my town.

Fare thee well sweet Anna Liffey, I can no longer stay,
And watch the new glass cages that spring up along the Quay.
My mind's too full of memories, to old to hear new chimes,
I'm part of what was Dublin, in the rare ould times.

The Sally Gardens

The lyrics of this song were written by W.B. Yeats in 1889.
The air is that of 'The Maids of the Mountain Shore'.

Arrangement copyright Waltons Publications Ltd.

It was down by the Sal - ly— Gar - dens my— love and— I did
meet. She— passed the— Sal- ly— Gar - dens with— lit- tle— snow- white feet. She
bid me— take love— ea - sy, as the leaves grow— on— the— tree. But—
I being—young and— fool - ish, and with her did— not a - gree.

In a field down by the river my love and I did stand,
And on my leaning shoulder she laid her snow-white hand.
She bid me take life easy, as the grass grows on the weirs,
But I was young and foolish, and now am full of tears.
Repeat first verse:-

Boolavogue

P.J. McCall, born in Patrick St., Dublin of a Carlow father and a Wexford mother,
set lyrics, relating to the Rebellion of 1798, to an ancient Irish air.

Arrangement copyright Waltons Publications Ltd.

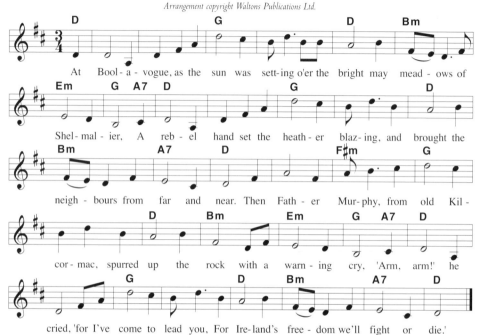

At Bool-a-vogue, as the sun was sett-ing o'er the bright may mead-ows of
Shel-mal-ier, A reb-el hand set the heath-er blaz-ing, and brought the
neigh-bours from far and near. Then Fath-er Mur-phy, from old Kil-
cor-mac, spurred up the rock with a warn-ing cry, 'Arm, arm!' he
cried, 'for I've come to lead you, For Ire-land's free-dom we'll fight or die.'

He led us on 'gainst the coming soldiers, and the cowardly yeomen we put to flight,
'Twas at the Barrow the boys of Wexford showed Bookey's regiment how men could fight.
Look out for hirelings, King George of England, search every kingdom where breathes a slave,
For Father Murphy of County Wexford sweeps o'er the land like a mighty wave.

We took Camolin and Enniscorthy, and Wexford storming drove out our foes.
'Twas at Slieve Coillte our pikes were reeking, with the crimson blood of the beaten Yeos.
At Tubberneering and Ballyellis, full many a Hessian lay in his gore.
Ah! Father Murphy, had aid come over, the green flag floated from shore to shore.

At Vinegar Hill o'er the pleasant Slaney, our heroes vainly stood back to back,
And the Yeos of Tullow took Father Murphy, and burned his body upon the rack.
God grant you glory, brave Father Murphy, and open heaven to all your men.
The cause that called you may call tomorrow, in another fight for the Green again.

4

The Nightingale

This English folksong, popular in Ireland, tells the story of a
meeting between a young girl and a married soldier.

Arrangement copyright Waltons Publications Ltd.

As— I went a-walk ing one morn-ing in May.— I met a young coup-le who
fond-ly did stray.— And one was a young— maid so sweet and so fair,— And the
oth-er one was a sol-dier and a brave gren-a-dier. And they kissed so sweet and
com-fort-ing as they clung to each oth-er.— They went arm in arm a-
long the road like sis-ter and bro-ther.— They went arm in arm a-long the road till they
came to a stream.— And they both sat down to-ge-ther for to hear the night-in-gale sing.—

And out of his knapsack he took a fine fiddle,
And he played her such a merry tune as you ever did hear.
And he played her such a merry tune as the valleys did ring,
And they both sat down together for to hear the nightingale sing.
Chorus:- (repeat after each verse)

'Oh soldier, Oh soldier, will you marry me?'
'Oh no,' said the soldier, 'that never can be,
For I have my own wife at home, in my own counteree,
And she is the sweetest little thing that ever you did see.'

'Now I'm off to India for seven long years,
Drinking wines and strong whiskey instead of cool beers.
And if I ever return again it'll be in the spring,
And we'll both sit down together and hear the nightingale sing.'

The Banks of My Own Lovely Lee

This tune has become the anthem of Cork. J. C. Shanahan wrote the music, with lyrics supposedly written by John Fitzgerald (they were later found in a letter from an Irish American whose identity remains unknown).

Copyright Shanahan

How— oft do my thoughts in their fan - cy take flight, To the home of my child- hood aw - ay.— To the days when each Pa - tri - ot's vi - sion seem'd bright, Ere I dream'd that those joys should de - cay.— When my heart was as light as the wild winds that blow, Down the Mar- dyke through each elm— tree— Where I sport - ed and played 'neath each green leaf - y shade, On the banks of my own love - ly Lee.— Where I sport - ed and played, 'neath each green leaf - y shade, on the banks of my own love - ly Lee.—

And then in the springtime of laughter and song,
Can I ever forget the sweet hours
With the friends of my youth as we rambled along
'Mongst the green mossy banks and wild flowers.
Then too, when the evening sun sinking to rest
Sheds its golden light over the sea,
The maid with her lover the wild daisies pressed
On the banks of my own lovely Lee,
The maid with her lover the wild daisies pressed
On the banks of my own lovely Lee.

'Tis a beautiful land, this dear isle of song,
Its gems shed their light to the world.
And her faithful sons bore thro' ages of wrong,
The standard St. Patrick unfurled.
Oh! would I were there with the friends I love best
And my fond bosom's partner with me.
We'd roam thy banks over, and when weary we'd rest
By thy waters, my own lovely Lee,
We'd roam thy banks over, and when weary we'd rest

By thy waters, my own lovely Lee.
Oh what joys should be mine ere this life should decline
To seek shells on thy sea-gilded shore.
While the steel-feathered eagle, oft splashing the brine
Brings longing for freedom once more.
Oh all that on earth I wish for or crave
Is that my last crimson drop be for thee,
To moisten the grass of my forefathers' grave
On the banks of my own lovely Lee,
To moisten the grass of my forefathers' grave
On the banks of my own lovely Lee.

The River Lee, Cork

The Mountains of Mourne

The lyrics of this beautiful ballad were written by Percy French (1854-1920) and sent to Houston Collison on the back of a postcard. Collison set them to the ancient Irish air, 'Carrigdhoun'.

Arrangement copyright Waltons Publications Ltd.

Oh Ma-ry this Lon-don's a won-der-ful sight, With the peo-ple here work-ing by day and by night. They don't sow po - ta-toes nor bar-ley nor wheat, But there's gangs of them dig-ging for gold in the street. At least when I asked them that's what I was told, So I just took a hand at this dig-ging for gold, But for all that I found there I might as well be, Where the moun-tains of Mourne sweep down to the sea.

I believe that when writing a wish you expressed
As to how the fine ladies in London were dressed.
Well if you believe me, when asked to a ball,
Faith, they don't wear a top to their dresses at all.
Oh, I've seen them myself and you could not in truth
Say if they were bound for a ball or a bath.
Don't be starting them fashions now, Mary Macree,
Where the mountains of Mourne sweep down to the sea.

I've seen England's king from the top of a bus,
I've never known him, tho' he means to know us,
And tho' by the Saxon we once were oppressed,
Still I cheered, God forgive me, I cheered with the rest.
And now that he's visited Erin's green shore,
We'll be much better friends than we've been heretofore.
When we've got all we want we're as quiet as can be,
Where the Mountains of Mourne sweep down to the sea.

You remember young Peter O'Loughlin of course,
Well, now he is here at the head of the Force.
I met him today, I was crossing the Strand,
And he stopped the whole street with one wave of his hand.
And there we stood talking of days that are gone,
While the whole population of London looked on.
But for all these great powers he's wishful, like me,
To be back where the dark Mourne sweeps down to the sea.

There's beautiful girls here – oh never you mind,
With beautiful shapes Nature never designed,
And lovely complexions, all roses and cream.
But O'Loughlin remarked with regard to the same,
That if at those roses you venture to sip,
The colours might all come away on your lip.
So I'll wait for the wild rose that's waiting for me,
Where the Mountains of Mourne sweep down to the sea.

9

Mourne Mountains, Newcastle, Co. Down

The Rose of Tralee

This song was written by William P. Mulchinock (1820-1862) for Mary O'Connor, a servant girl in his house with whom he fell in love. Forced to flee to England for a time, when he returned, Mary had died of consumption.

Arrangement copyright Waltons Publications Ltd.

Oh the pale moon was ri - sing a - bove the green moun- tain, The sun was de -
clin- ing be - neath the blue sea, When I strayed with my love o'er the pure cry- stal
foun- tain, that stands in the beau - ti - ful Vale of Tra - lee. She was
love - ly and fair as the rose in the Sum- mer, Yet 'twas not her
beau - ty a - lone that won me. Oh no, 'twas the truth in her
eyes e - ver dawn- ing, That made me love Ma - ry, the Rose of Tra - lee.

The cool shades of evening their mantles were spreading,
And Mary, all smiling, sat listening to me.
The moon thro' the valley her pale rays was shedding,
When I won the heart of the Rose of Tralee.
Tho' lovely and fair as the rose of the summer,
Yet 'twas not her beauty alone that won me.
Oh! no, 'twas the truth in her eye ever dawning,
That made me love Mary, the Rose of Tralee.

Raglan Road

Patrick Kavanagh wrote this great poem, situated on Raglan Road in Ballsbridge, Dublin,
and set it to the famous air, 'Fáinne Geal an Lae' ('The Dawning of the Day').

By kind permission of the Trustees of the Estate of Patrick Kavavagh, c/o Peter Fallon, Literary Agent.

On Grafton Street in November we tripped lightly along the ledge
Of a deep ravine where can be seen the worth of passion's pledge.
The Queen of Hearts still making tarts, and I not making hay.
Oh, I loved too much and by such and such is happiness thrown away.

I gave her gifts of the mind, I gave her the secret sign that's known
To the artists who have known the true gods of sound and stone
And words and tint. I did not stint for I gave her poems to say,
With her own name there and her own dark hair like clouds over fields of May.

On a quiet street where old ghosts meet I see her walking now
Away from me so hurriedly, my reason must allow
That I had wooed not as I should a creature made of clay.
When the angel woos the clay he'll lose his wings at the dawn of day.

A Bunch of Thyme

A simple song about the loss of innocence, thyme a symbol for virginity.

Arrangement copyright Waltons Publications Ltd.

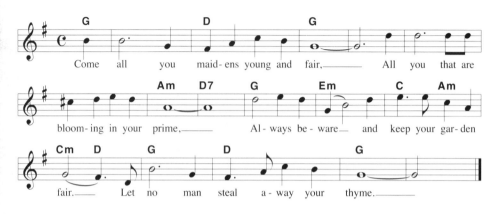

Come all you maid-ens young and fair,___ All you that are
bloom-ing in your prime,___ Al-ways be-ware___ and keep your gar-den
fair.___ Let no man steal a-way your thyme.___

Gathering the Peat

Chorus:
For thyme, it is a precious thing,
And thyme brings all things to my mind.
Thyme with all its flavours,
Along with all its joys,
Thyme brings all things to my mind.

Once I had a bunch of thyme,
I thought it never would decay.
Then came a lusty sailor,
Who chanced to pass my way,
And stole my bunch of thyme away.
Chorus:-

The sailor gave to me a rose,
A rose that never would decay.
He gave it to me,
To keep me reminded
Of when he stole my thyme away.
Chorus:-

Churnin

The Juice of the Barley

Traditional

Arrangement copyright Waltons Publications Ltd.

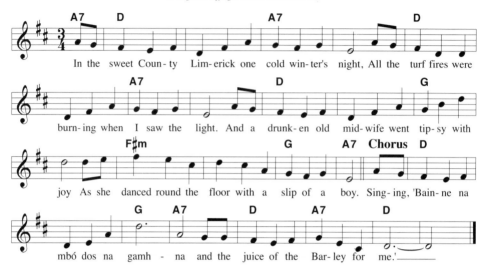

In the sweet Coun- ty Lim- erick one cold win- ter's night, All the turf fires were burn- ing when I saw the light. And a drunk- en old mid- wife went tip- sy with joy As she danced round the floor with a slip of a boy. Sing- ing, 'Bain- ne na mbó dos na gamh - na and the juice of the Bar- ley for me.'

Well when I was a gossoon of eight years or so,
With me turf and me primer to school I did go,
To a drafty old schoolhouse without any door,
Where lay the schoolmaster blind drunk on the floor.
Chorus:- (repeat after each verse)

At the learning I was no great genius I'm thinking,
But I soon bet the master entirely at drinking.
Not a wake nor a wedding for five miles around,
But meself in the corner was sure to be found.

One Sunday the priest read me out from the altar,
Saying, 'You'll end up your days with your neck in a halter,
And you'll dance a fine jig between heaven and hell.'
And his words they did frighten me, the truth for to tell.

So the very next morning as the dawn it did break,
I went down to the vestry, the pledge for to take,
And there, 'pon my soul, after eating his lunch,
By a big roaring fire sat the priest drinking punch.

Well from that day to this I have wandered alone,
I'm Jack of all trades and a master of none,
With the sky for me roof and the earth for me floor,
And I'll dance out me days drinking whiskey galore.

14

O'Donnell Abú

The song originally appeared in *The Nation* newspaper in 1843 as
'The Clanconnell War Song'. It was written by Michael Joseph McCann, from Galway.
Arrangement copyright Waltons Publications Ltd.

Proud-ly the note of the trum-pet is sound-ing,— Loud-ly the war cries a-
rise on the gale. Fleet-ly the steed by Lough Swil-ly is bound-ing To
join the thick squad - rons on Saim - er's green vale. On, ev-'ry moun-tain-eer,
stran - gers to flight and fear, Rush to the stand - ard of
daunt-less Red Hugh. Bon - naught and Gal-low-glass, throng from each
moun-tain pass,— On - ward for Er - in, O' Don - nell A - bú!

Princely O'Neill to our aid is advancing,
With many a chieftain and warrior clan.
A thousand proud steeds in his vanguard are
  prancing,
'Neath the borderers brave from the banks of
  the Bann.
Many a heart shall quail under its coat of mail,
Deeply the merciless foeman shall rue,
When on his ear shall ring, borne on the
  breeze's wing,
Tir Connell's dread war cry, 'O'Donnell Abú!'

Wildly o'er Desmond the war wolf is howling,
Fearless the eagle sweeps over the plain.
The fox in the streets of the city is prowling,
And all who would scare them are banished or
  slain.
On with O'Donnell, then, fight the old fight
  again,
Sons of Tir Connell are valiant and true.
Make the proud Saxon feel Erin's avenging
  steel,
Strike for your country, O'Donnell Abú!

15

The Minstrel Boy

This battle song, set to the air of 'The Moreen', was written
by Thomas Moore, more often a writer of love songs.

Arrangement copyright Waltons Publications Ltd.

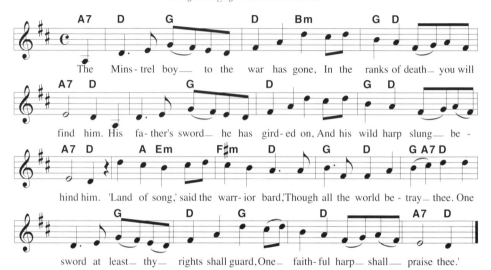

The Mins-trel boy— to the war has gone, In the ranks of death— you will
find him. His fa-ther's sword— he has gird-ed on, And his wild harp slung— be -
hind him. 'Land of song,' said the warr-ior bard,'Though all the world be - tray— thee. One
sword at least— thy— rights shall guard,One— faith-ful harp— shall— praise thee.'

The Minstrel fell! – but the foeman's chain could not bring his proud soul under.
The harp he loved ne'er spoke again, for he tore its chords asunder,
And said, 'No chains shall sully thee, thou soul of love and bravery!
Thy songs were made for the pure and free, they shall never sound in slavery.'

Milk for the Creamery

16

Four Green Fields

This song was written by Tommy Makem. The old woman in the song is Ireland,
and her four sons are the four Provinces: Ulster, Munster, Leinster and Connaught.

Copyright Tin Whistle Music Ltd.

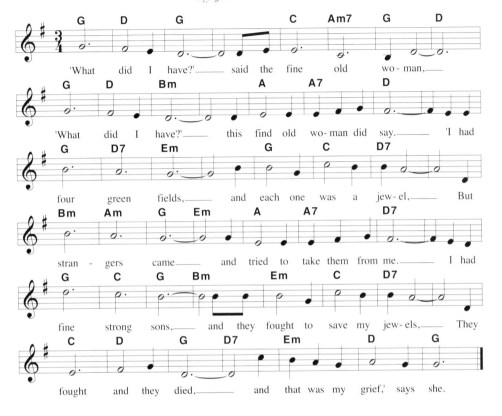

'Long time ago,' said the fine old woman,
'Long time ago,' the fine old woman did say,
'There was war and death, plundering and pillage,
My children starved in mountain, valley and sea,
And their wailing cries, they shook the very heavens,
My four green fields ran red with their blood,' said she.

'What have I now,' said the fine old woman,
'What have I now,' this proud old woman did say,
'I have four green fields and one of them's in bondage,
In strangers' hands, who tried to take it from me.
But my sons have sons, as brave as were their fathers,
My four green fields will bloom once again,' said she.

I'm a Rover

This Scottish ballad, popular in Ireland, tells the simple
story of a young girl and her ploughman lover.

Arrangement copyright Waltons Publications Ltd.

I'm a rov - er and sel - dom so - ber, I'm a
ro ver of high— de-gree.——— It's when I'm drink - ing I'm
al - ways think - ing how to gain my— love's com - pa - ny.———

Though the night be as dark as dungeon, not a star to be seen above,
I will be guided without a stumble, into the arms of my own true love.

He stepped up to her bedroom window, kneeling gently upon a stone,
He rapped at her bedroom window, 'Darling dear, do you lie alone?'

'It's only me, your own true lover, open the door and let me in,
For I have come on a long journey and I'm near drenched to the skin.'

She opened the door with the greatest pleasure, she opened the door and she let him in.
They both shook hands and embraced each other, until the morning they lay as one.

The cocks were crowing, the birds were whistling, the streams they ran free about the brae.
'Remember lass, I'm a ploughman laddie, and the farmer I must obey.'

'Now my love, I must go and leave thee, and though the hills they are high above,
I will climb them with greater pleasure, since I've been in the arms of my love.'

Paddy's Green Shamrock Shore

Traditional

Arrangement copyright Waltons Publications Ltd.

Our ship she lies at anchor, she's standing by the quay.
May fortune bright shine down each night, as we sail over the sea.
Many ships were lost, many lives it cost, on the journey that lay before.
With a tear in my eye, I'm bidding goodbye to Paddy's Green Shamrock Shore.

So fare thee well my own true love, I'll think of you night and day,
And a place in my mind you surely will find, although I am so far away.
Though I'll be alone far away from my home, I'll think of the good times once more,
Until the day I can make my way back to Paddy's Green Shamrock Shore.

And now the ship is on the waves, may heaven protect us all.
With the wind in the sail, we surely can't fail on this voyage to Baltimore.
But my parents and friends did wait till the end, till I could see them no more,
I then took a chance for to glance at Paddy's Green Shamrock Shore.

Slievenamon

This song was written by Charles J. Kickham, who was born in County Tipperary in 1828,
and died in Dublin in 1882. The title, translated, means 'Woman of the Mountain'.

Arrangement copyright Waltons Publications Ltd.

It was not the grace of her queenly air, nor her cheek of the rose's glow,
Nor her soft black eyes, nor her flowing hair, nor was it her lily-white brow.
'Twas the sound of truth and of melting ruth, and the smile like a summer dawn,
That stole my heart away, on a soft summer day, in the valley near Slievenamon.

In the festive hall, by the wave-washed shore, oh my restless spirit cries,
'My love, oh my love, shall I ne'er see you more? And my land, will you never uprise?'
By night and by day, I ever, ever pray, while lonely my life flows on,
To see our flag unfurled and my true-love to enfold, in the valley near Slievenamon.

Cockles and Mussels

The author of this famous Dublin song is unknown. Cockles, mussels and other fresh fish were sold by 'Dealers' (Hawkers) from three-wheeled carts, often made from wicker.

Arrangement copyright Waltons Publications Ltd.

She was a fishmonger, but sure 'twas no wonder,
For so were her father and mother before.
And they both wheeled their barrow
Through streets broad and narrow,
Crying cockles and mussels, alive alive O!
Chorus:-

She died of a fever, and no one could save her,
And that was the end of sweet Mollie Malone.
But her ghost wheels her barrow
Through streets broad and narrow,
Crying cockles and mussels, alive alive O!
Chorus:-

The Shores of Amerikay

Emigration is a theme common in Irish songs of the 19th century –
America being the primary target of the emigrants.
Arrangement copyright Waltons Publications Ltd.

It's not for the want of employment I'm going, it's not for the love of fame,
That fortune bright may shine over me, and give me a glorious name.
It's not for the want of employment I'm going, o'er the weary and stormy sea,
But to seek a home for my own true-love, on the shores of Amerikay.

And when I am bidding my last farewell, the tears like rain will blind,
To think of my friends in my own native land, and the home I'm leaving behind.
But if I'm to die on a foreign land, and be buried so far away,
No fond mother's tears will be shed o'er my grave, on the shores of Amerikay.

Muirsheen Durkin

The air to this song comes from 'Cailíní Deas Mhuigheo' ('The Beautiful Girls of Wexford').

Arrangement copyright Waltons Publications Ltd.

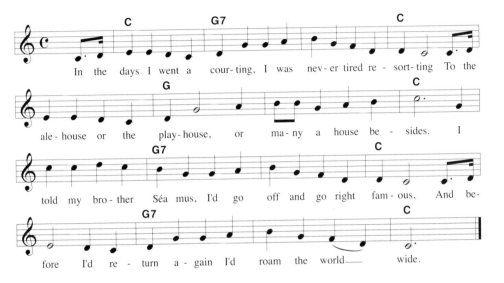

In the days I went a cour- ting, I was nev- er tired re - sort- ting To the
ale - house or the play- house, or ma- ny a house be - sides. I
told my bro - ther Séa mus, I'd go off and go right fam - ous, And before I'd re - turn a - gain I'd roam the world____ wide.

Chorus:-
So goodbye Muirsheen Durkin, I'm sick and tired of working,
No more I'll dig the praties, no longer I'll be fooled.
As sure as me name is Carney, I'll go off to California,
Where instead of diggin' praties, I'll be diggin' lumps of gold.

I've courted girls in Blarney, in Kanturk and in Killarney,
In Passage and in Queenstown, that is the Cobh of Cork.
So goodbye to all this pleasure, for I'm going to take me leisure,
And the next time you will hear from me, will be a letter from New York.
Chorus:-

Goodbye to all the boys at home, I'm sailing far across the foam
To try and make me fortune in far Amerikay.
There's gold and money plenty for the poor and for the gentry,
And when I come back again I never more will stray.
Chorus:-

Spancil Hill

Written by Michael Considine, who emigrated to America in 1870.
Spancil Hill is a cross-roads four miles from Ennis, Co. Clare.

Arrangement copyright Waltons Publications Ltd.

Last night as I lay dream - ing of pleas - ant days gone by,——

—— My mind being bent on ramb - ling to Ire-land I— did fly.——

—— I stepped on board a vis - ion and foll- owed with— a will,——

—— Till I late- ly came to an-chor at the cross— near Span - cil Hill.——

Delighted by the novelty, enchanted with the scene,
Where in my early boyhood there often I had been,
I thought I heard a murmur and I think I hear it still,
It's the little stream of water that flows down Spancil Hill.

To amuse a passing fancy, I lay down on the ground,
And all my school companions they shortly gathered round.
When we were home returning, we danced with bright goodwill,
To Martin Moynahan's music at the cross at Spancil Hill.

It was on the twenty-third of June, the day before the fair,
When Ireland's sons and daughters in crowds assembled there.
The young, the old, the brave and the bold came, their duty to fulfil,
At the parish church in Clooney, a mile from Spancil Hill.

I went to see my neighbours, to hear what they might say,
The old ones they were dead and gone, the young ones turning grey.
I met the tailor Quigley, he as bold as ever still,
For he used to make my britches when I lived at Spancil Hill.

I paid a flying visit to my first and only love,
She's as fair as any lily and gentle as a dove.
She threw her arms around me, crying, 'Johnny I love you still!'
She was a farmer's daughter, the pride of Spancil Hill.

Well I dreamt I hugged and kissed her as in the days of yore.
She said, 'Johnny you're only joking, as many the time before.'
The cock crew in the morning, he crew both loud and shrill,
And I woke in California, many miles from Spancil Hill.

Irish Hay Carts

The Rose of Mooncoin

This beautiful love song, written by Seamus Kavanagh, is set in Mooncoin, Co. Kilkenny.

Copyright Waltons Publications Ltd.

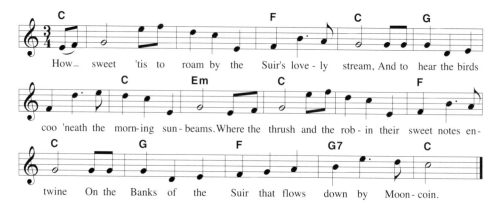

How_ sweet 'tis to roam by the Suir's love-ly stream, And to hear the birds coo 'neath the morn-ing sun-beams. Where the thrush and the rob-in their sweet notes en-twine On the Banks of the Suir that flows down by Moon-coin.

Chorus:
Flow on lovely river, flow gently along,
By your waters so sweet sounds the lark's merry song.
On your green banks I'll wander where first I did join
With you, lovely Molly, the Rose of Mooncoin.

Oh! Molly, dear Molly, it breaks my fond heart
To know that we two forever must part.
I'll think of you, Molly, while sun and moon shine,
On the banks of the Suir that flows down by Mooncoin.
Chorus:-

She has sailed far away o'er the dark rolling foam,
Far away from the hills of her dear Irish home,
Where the fisherman sports with his small boat and line,
On the banks of the Suir that flows down by Mooncoin.
Chorus:-

Then here's to the Suir with its valleys so fair,
As oft' times we wandered in the cool morning air,
Where the roses are blooming and lilies entwine,
On the banks of the Suir that flows down by Mooncoin.
Chorus:-

The Irish Rover

Written by Joseph Crofts

Copyright Waltons Publications Ltd.

There was Barney Magee from the banks of the Lee,
There was Hogan from Co. Tyrone.
There was Johnny McGurk who was scared stiff of work,
And a chap from Westmeath named Malone.
There was slugger O'Toole who was drunk as a rule,
And fighting Bill Tracy from Dover,
And your man Mick McCann from the banks of the Bann
Was the skipper on the Irish Rover.

We had one million bags of the best Sligo bags,
We had two million bags of bone.
We had three million bales of nanny goats' tails,
We had four million barrels of stone.
We had five million hogs, we had six million dogs,
And seven million barrels of porter.
We had eight million sides of old blind horse's hides,
In the hold of the Irish Rover.

We had sailed seven years, when the measles broke out,
And our ship lost her way in a fog.
And the whole of the crew was reduced down to two,
'Twas myself and the captain's old dog.
Then the ship struck a rock, O Lord what a shock,
And nearly tumbled over,
Turned nine times around, then the poor old dog was drowned,
I'm the last of the Irish Rover.

The Square and Cathedral, Queenstown (now Cobh), Co. Cork

I Once Loved a Lass

This beautiful Scottish love song tells of the impossible riddles of love.
Arrangement copyright Waltons Publications Ltd.

I once loved a lass, and I loved her so well,____
____ That I hat-ed all oth-ers that spoke of her ill,____
____ But now she's re-ward-ed me well for my love.____
____ She's— gone to be wed to an-oth-er.____

When I saw my love go through the church door,
With bride and bride maidens, they made a fine show,
And I followed the man with my heart full of woe,
For now she is wed to another.

When I saw my love a-sit down to dine,
I sat down beside her and I poured out the wine,
And I drank to the lass that should have been mine,
But now she is wed to another.

The men of yon forest, they ask it of me,
How many strawberries grow in the salt sea?
And I ask of them back with a tear in my eye,
How many ships sail in the forest?

So dig me a grave and dig it so deep,
And cover it over with flowers so sweet,
And I'll turn in, for to take a long sleep,
And maybe in time I'll forget her.

So they dug him a grave and they dug it so deep,
They covered it over with flowers so sweet.
And he's turned in for to take a long sleep,
And maybe by now he's forgotten.

A Kerry Milkmaid

I Know My Love

A simple story of a woman spurned and the anguish she feels as her lover entertains other women.

Arrangement copyright Waltons Publications Ltd.

I know my love by his way of walk - ing, And I
know my love by his way of talk - ing, And I know my love dressed
in his jer - sey blue, And if my love leaves me, what will I

Chorus
do?___ And still she cried, 'I love him the best, and a
troub - led mind can__ know no rest.'___ And still she cried,
'Bonn - y boys are few, And if my love leaves me, what will I do?'

There is a dance house down in Mardyke,
And 'tis there my true-love goes every night,
And he takes a strange one upon his knee,
And don't you think now that vexes me?
Chorus:-

If my love knew I could wash and wring,
And if my love knew I could weave and spin,
I'd make for him a suit of the finest kind,
But the want of money leaves me behind.
Chorus:-

Matt Hyland

Traditional

Arrangement copyright Waltons Publications Ltd.

So straightaway to her love she goes, into his chamber to awake him,
Saying, 'Arise my love and go away, this very night you will be taken.
I overheard my father say, in spite of me he would transport you,
So arise my love, and go away, I wish to God I'd gone before you.'

They both sat down upon the bed, just for the side of one half hour,
And not a word by either said, as down their cheeks the tears did shower.
She laid her hand upon his breast, around his neck her arms entwined.
'Not a duke nor lord nor an earl I'll wed, I'll wait for you, my own Matt Hyland.'

The lord discoursed with his daughter fair, one night alone in her chamber,
Saying, 'We'll give you leave for to bring him back, since there's no one can win your favour.'
She wrote a letter then in haste, her heart for him was still repining.
They brought him back, to the church they went, and made a lord of young Matt Hyland.

Roadside Butter Market

My Cavan Girl

American-born Thom Moore won the Cavan Song Contest with this song.
Copyright Thom Moore (MCPS)

As I walk the road from Kil- la - shan - dra, wea- ry I___ sit down, For it's twelve long miles a - round the lake, to get to Ca- van town, Lough Ough- ter and the___ road I go, once seemed be - yond com - pare. Now I curse the time it takes to reach my Ca- van girl__ so fair.

The autumn shades are on the leaves, the trees will soon be bare,
And each red coat leaf around me seems the colour of her hair
My gaze retreats, defies my feet and once again I sigh,
For a broken pool of sky reminds, the colour of her eyes.

At the Cavan cross each Sunday morning, it's there she can be found,
And she seems to have the eye of every boy in Cavan town.
If my luck will hold I'll have the golden summer of her smile,
And to break the hearts of Cavan men she'll talk to me awhile.

So next Sunday evening finds me homeward Killeshandra bound,
To work a week till I return to court in Cavan town.
When if she would be my bride at least she'd not said no,
So next Sunday morning 'rouse myself and back to her I go.

Sliabh Gallion Braes

An exile song associated with Slieve Gallion Braes, a highland
on the Sperrin mountains in counties Derry and Tyrone.

Arrangement copyright Waltons Publications Ltd.

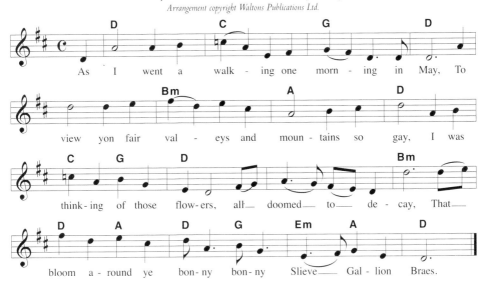

As I went a walk - ing one morn - ing in May, To
view yon fair val - eys and moun - tains so gay, I was
think - ing of those flow - ers, all— doomed— to— de - cay, That—
bloom a - round ye bon - ny bon - ny Slieve— Gal - lion Braes.

How oft in the morning with my dog and my gun,
I roam through the glens for joy and for fun,
But those days are now all over, and I must go away,
So farewell unto ye, bonny bonny Sliabh Gallion Braes.

How oft of an evening and the sun in the West,
I roved hand in hand with the one I loved best,
But the hopes of youth are vanished, and now I'm far away,
So farewell unto ye, bonny bonny Sliabh Gallion Braes.

Oh! it was not the want of employment at home
That caused us poor exiles in sorrow to roam,
But those tyrannising landlords, they would not let us stay,
So farewell unto ye, bonny bonny Sliabh Gallion Braes.

I Know Where I'm Going

An Ulster folksong collected by Herbert Hughes, expressing the wishes of
a young girl thinking of her love and who she will finally marry.

Arrangement copyright Waltons Publications Ltd.

I know where I'm go-ing,— and I know who's go-ing with me.

I know who I love, but the dear knows who I'll mar - ry.

I have stockings of silk, shoes of fine green leather,
Combs to bind my hair, and a ring for every finger.

Feather beds are soft and painted rooms are bonny,
But I would leave them all to go with my love Johnny.

Some say he's dark, I say he's bonny,
He's the fairest of them all, my handsome, winsome Johnny.

I know where I'm going, and I know who's going with me,
I know who I love, but the dear knows who I'll marry.

Lisdoonvarna, Co. Clare, Famous for Its Matchmaking Festival

Black Is the Colour

Traditional

Arrangement copyright Waltons Publications Ltd.

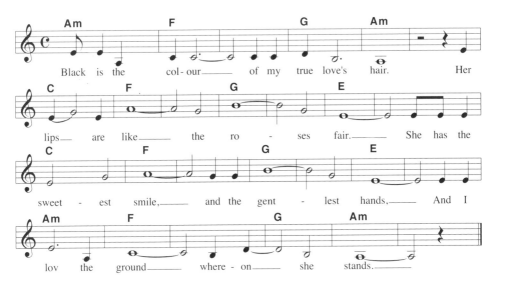

Black is the col-our of my true love's hair. Her
lips are like the ro - ses fair. She has the
sweet - est smile, and the gent - lest hands, And I
lov the ground where - on she stands.

I love my love and well she knows, I love the ground whereon she goes.
I wish the day it soon would come, when she and I could be as one.

I go to the Clyde and I mourn and weep, for satisfied I ne'er can be.
I write her a letter, just a few short lines, and suffer death a thousand times.

The Irish Forge

A Bucket of Mountain Dew

This song was written by Samuel Lover (1797-1869), the son of a stockbroker.

Arrangement copyright Waltons Publications Ltd.

Let grass-es grow and wat-ers flow in a free and eas-y way, But give me en-ough of the rare old stuff that's made near Gal-way Bay. And gau-gers all from Don-e-gal, Sli-go and Lei-trim too, We'll give them the slip and we'll take a sip of the real old Moun-tain Dew. With me di-the-ry al the dal and me di-the-ry al the dal, With me do-ri di-the-ry al day. With me di-the-ry al the dal and me di-the-ry al the dal, And me do-ri di-th-ry al day.

There's a neat little still at the foot of the hill, where the smoke curls up to the sky.
By a whiff of the smell you can plainly tell, that there's poitín boys close by.
For it fills the air with a perfume rare, and betwixt both me and you,
As home we roll, we drink a bowl, or a bucketful of mountain dew.

Now learned men as use the pen have writ the praises high
Of the rare poitín from Ireland green, distilled from wheat and rye.
Away with your pills, it'll cure all ills, be ye pagan, Christian or Jew,
So take off your coat and grease your throat, with a bucketful of mountain dew.

Come Back Paddy Reilly

Words & Music by Percy French

Arrangement copyright Waltons Publications Ltd.

The gar-den of E-den has van-ished they say, But I know the lie of it still._____ Just turn to the left at the bridge of Finn - ay, And stop when half way to Coot - hill._____ 'Tis there you will find it, I know sure e - nough, When for-tune shall ans - wer my call,_____ For the grass it grows green a - round Ball - y - james - duff, And the blue sky hangs o - ver it all._____ And tones that are ten-der, and tones that are rough Come whis - per - ing o - ver the sea,_____ Come back Pad-dy Reil - ly to Bal - ly - james - duff, Come home Pad-dy Reil- ly to me._____

My mother once told me that when I was born, the day that I first saw the light,
I looked down the street on that very first morn, and gave a great crow of delight.
Now most new-born babies appear in a huff, and start with a sorrowful squall,
But I knew I was born in Ballyjamesduff, and that's why I smiled at them all.
The baby's a man now, he's toil-worn and tough, still whispers come over the sea,
Come back Paddy Reilly to Ballyjamesduff, come home Paddy Reilly to me.

The night that we danced by the light of the moon, with Phil to the fore with his flute,
When Phil threw his lip over 'Come Again Soon', he'd dance the foot out o' yer boot.
That day that I took long Magee by the scruff, for slanderin' Rosie Kilrain,
Then marchin' him straight out of Ballyjamesduff, assisted him into a drain.
Oh, sweet are me dreams as the dudeen I puff, of whisperings over the sea,
Come back Paddy Reilly to Ballyjamesduff, come home Paddy Reilly to me.

Kate Kearney's Cottage, Killarney, Co. Kerry

Carrigdhoun

The lyrics of this song, sung to a traditional air, were written by Cork-born poet Denny Lane. It deals with the flight to France of one of the 'Wild Geese'. The air is very similar to 'The Mountains of Mourne'.

Arrangement copyright Waltons Publications Ltd.

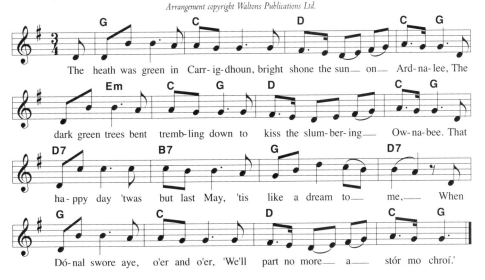

The heath was green in Carr-ig-dhoun, bright shone the sun— on— Ard-na-lee, The
dark green trees bent tremb-ling down to kiss the slum-ber-ing— Ow-na-bee. That
ha-ppy day 'twas but last May, 'tis like a dream to— me,— When
Dó-nal swore aye, o'er and o'er, 'We'll part no more— a— stór mo chroí.'

On Carrigdhoun the heath is brown, the clouds are dark o'er Ardnalee,
And many a stream comes rushing down to swell the angry Ownabee.
The moaning blast is sweeping fast, through many a leafless tree,
And I'm alone for he is gone, my hawk is flown, ochón mo chroí.

Soft April showers and bright May flowers will bring the summer back again.
But will they bring me back the hours I spent with my brave Dónal then?
'Tis but a chance, for he's gone to France, to wear the fleur-de-lis.
But I'll follow you, my Dónal Dhu for still I'm true to you, a chroí.

41

Teddy O'Neill

Words & Music by Shamus O'Leary

Arrangement copyright Waltons Publications Ltd.

I dreamt but last night, oh! bad luck to my dream-ing, I'd
die if I thought 'twould come sure-ly to pass. But I dreamt, while the tears down my
pi - llow were strea-ming that Te - ddy was cour-ting a - no-ther fair lass. Och
did I not wake with a wee-ping and wai-ling, The grief of that thought was too
deep to con-ceal; My mo - ther cried 'No-ra, child what is your ail-ing?' But
all I could ans - wer was 'Te - ddy O' Neill.'

I've come to the cabin he danced his wild jigs in,
As neat a mud palace as ever was seen,
And considering it served to keep poultry and pigs in,
I'm sure it was always most elegant clean.
But now all about it seems lonely and dreary,
All sad and all silent, no piper, no reel;
Not even the sun thro' the casement is cheery,
Since I miss the dear darling boy, Teddy O'Neill.

Shall I ever forget when the big ship was ready,
The moment had come when my love must depart,
How I sobb'd like a spaleen, 'Good-bye to you, Teddy',
With drops on my cheeks and a stone at my heart.
He says it's to better his fortune he's roving,
But what would be gold to the joy I would feel,
I saw him come back to me honest and loving,
Still poor, but my own darling, Teddy O'Neill.

All for Me Grog

This old song is a celebration of the three vices, wine, women and song, and the cost of over indulgence.

Arrangement copyright Waltons Publications Ltd.

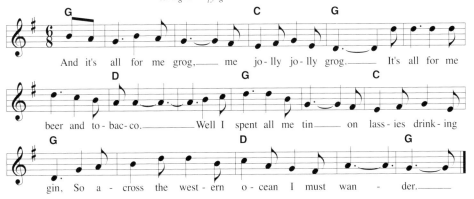

And it's all for me grog,___ me jo-lly jo-lly grog.___ It's all for me
beer and to-bac-co._____Well I spent all me tin___ on lass-ies drink-ing
gin, So a-cross the west-ern o-cean I must wan - der.___

Where are me boots, me noggin' noggin' boots?
They're all gone for beer and tobacco.
For the heels they are worn out and the toes are kicked about,
And the soles are looking out for better weather.

Where is me shirt, me noggin' noggin' shirt?
It's all gone for beer and tobacco.
For the collar is all worn, and the sleeves they are all torn,
And the tail is looking out for better weather.

I'm sick in the head and I haven't been to bed,
Since first I came ashore from me slumber.
For I spent all me dough on the lassies, don't you know,
Far across the Western ocean I must wander.

The Auld Orange Flute

The words to this popular Northern Ireland song were written by Nugent Bohem
and set to the old air 'Toor-a-Lay'.

Arrangement copyright Waltons Publications Ltd.

In the Coun-ty Ty - rone near the town of Dun - gan non there were ma-ny a
ruc-tion me - self had a hand in. Bob Will-iams who lived there, a weav-er by trade, and
all of us thought him a stout Or-ange blade. On the twelfth of Ju - ly as it year-ly did
come, Bob played on his flute to the sound of the drum, You may talk of your
harp your pi - an - o or lute, But no-thing could sound like this auld Or-ange flute.

But this treacherous scoundrel, he took us all in,
For he married a Papish, called Bridget McGinn,
Turned Papish himself, and forsook the old cause,
That gave us our freedom, religion, and laws.
Now the boys in the townland made noise upon it
And Bob had to fly to the Province of Connaught.
He flew with his wife and fixings to boot,
And along with the others, his ould Orange flute.

At chapel on Sundays, to atone for past deeds,
He'd say Pater and Aves, and counted his beads,
Till after some time, at the priest's own desire
He went with that ould flute to play in the choir.
He went with the ould flute to play in the loft,
But the instrument shivered and sighed and then coughed.
When he blew it and fingered it, it made a strange noise,
For the flute would play only 'The Protestant Boys'.

Easy and Slow

In this song the young couple set out from Christ Church and head westward to the Phoenix Park, a short distance away. This old Dublin song was given new words by Sean O'Casey for his play *Red Roses for Me.*

Arrangement copyright Waltons Publications Ltd.

All along Thomas Street, down to the Liffey,
The sun was gone down and the evening grew dark.
Along by King's Bridge and begod in a jiffey,
Me arms were around her beyond in the park.
Chorus:- (repeat after each verse)

From city or country, a girl's a jewel,
And well known for gripping it most of them are.
But any young fella is really a fool,
If he tries for the first time, to go a bit far.

And if ever you go to the town of Dungannon,
You can search till your eyeballs are empty and blind.
Be yeh lyin' or walkin' or sittin' or runnin',
A girl like Annie you never will find.

A Nation Once Again

This song was written by one of the founder members of the Young Ireland Movement, Thomas Davis (1814-45). It reflects the patriotism of its author and his great friends Daniel O'Connell and John Mitchel.

Arrangement copyright Waltons Publications Ltd.

And from that time through wildest woe, that hope has shone a far light,
Nor could love's brightest summer glow, outshine that solemn starlight.
It seemed to watch above my head, in forum, field and fane,
Its angel voice sang round my bed, 'a nation once again.'

It whisper'd too that freedom's ark and service high and holy,
Would be profaned by feelings dark and passions vain or lowly.
For freedom comes from God's right hand and needs a godly train,
And righteous men must make our land a nation once again.

So as I grew from boy to man, I bent me to that bidding,
My spirit of each selfish plan and cruel passion ridding.
For thus I hoped some day to aid, oh! can such hope be vain?
When my dear country shall be made a nation once again!

The Waxies Dargle

The waxies (candle makers) held an annual outing to the seaside town
of Bray, Co. Wicklow, 12 miles (20 km) south of Dublin.

Arrangement copyright Waltons Publications Ltd.

Says_ my oul wan to your oul wan 'will you come to the Wax-ies Dar-gle?' Says_ your oul wan to my oul wan 'sure I have-n't got a far thing.' I've just been down to Mon-to Town To see young Kill Mc - Ar-dle, But he would-n't give me a half a crown To go to the Wax-ies Dar-gle'. What will you have, will you have a pint? I'll have a pint with you sir, And if one of you does-n't or-der soon We'll be thrown out of the booz-er.

Says my aul' wan to your aul' wan,
'Will you come to Galway Races?'
Says your aul' wan to my aul' wan,
'With the price of my aul' lad's braces.
I went down to Capel Street,
To the Jew man moneylenders,
But they wouldn't give me a couple of bob
On my oul' lad's suspenders.'
Chorus:- (repeat after each verse)

Says my aul' wan to your aul' wan,
'We have no beef or mutton,
But if we go down to Monto Town,
We might get a drink for nuttin'.
Here's a piece of advice
I got from an aul' fishmonger,
When food is scarce, and you see the hearse,
You'll know you have died of hunger.'

47

The Humour Is on Me Now

Traditional

Arrangement copyright Waltons Publications Ltd.

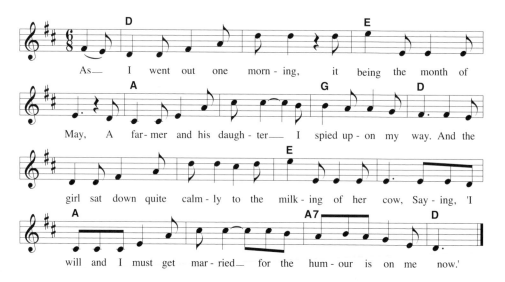

As— I went out one morn - ing, it being the month of May, A far-mer and his daugh - ter— I spied up - on my way. And the girl sat down quite calm - ly to the milk - ing of her cow, Say - ing, 'I will and I must get mar - ried— for the hum - our is on me now.'

'Ah, be quiet you foolish daughter, and hold your simple tongue,
You're better free and single and happy while you're young.'
But the daughter shook her shoulders and milked her patient cow,
Saying, 'I will and I must get married for the humour is on me now.'

'And sure, who are you to turn me, that married young yourself,
And took my darling mother from off the single shelf?'
'Ah sure, daughter dear, go aisy and milk your patient cow,
For a man may have his humour but the humour is off me now.'

'Well indeed, I'll tell my mother the awful things you say,
Indeed I'll tell my mother this very blessed day.'
'Och now, daughter, have a heart, dear, you'll start a fearful row.'
'So I will unless I marry for the humour is on me now.'

'Och, if you must be married will you tell me who's the man?'
And quickly she did answer, 'There's William, James and John,
A carpenter, a tailor, and a man to milk the cow,
For I will and I must get married and the humour is on me now.'

'A carpenter's a sharp man, and a tailor's hard to face,
With his legs across the table and his threads about the place,
And sure John's a fearful tyrant and never lacks a row,
But I will and I must be married for the humour is on me now.'

'Well if you must be married, will you tell me what you'll do?
'Sure I will,' the daughter answered, 'just the same as ma and you.
I'll be mistress of my dairy and my butter and my cow.'
'And your husband too, I'll venture, for the humour is on you now.'

So at last the daughter married and married well-to-do,
And loved her darling husband for a month, a year or two.
But John was all a tyrant and she quickly rued her vow,
Saying, 'I'm sorry that I married for the humour is off me now.'

Courting Couple, Blarney, Co. Cork

Follow Me up to Carlow

This song, written by P.J. McCall, celebrates the Battle of Glenmalure in 1580.

Arrangement copyright Waltons Publications Ltd.

Lift Mac-Ca-hir Óg your face, brood-ing o'er the old dis-grace, That
Black Fitz-Will-iam stormed your place, and drove you to the fern.
Grey said vic-to-ry was sure. Soon the fire-brand he'd se-cure,
Till he met at Glen-ma-lure with Fiach Mac-Hugh O' Byrne. Curse and swear,
Lord Kil-dare, Fiach will do what Fiach will dare, Now Fitz-Will-iam
have a care, fal-len is__ your star low. Up with hal-berd,
out with sword, on we'll go for by the Lord,
Fiach Mac-Hugh has giv-en the word, fol-low me up to Car-low.

See the swords of Glen Imaal, a flashing o'er the English pale,
See all the children of the Gael beneath O'Byrne's banner.
Rooster of a fighting stock, would yet let a saxon cock
Crow out upon an Irish rock, fly up and teach him manners.
Chorus:- (repeat after each verse)

Now from Tassagart to Clonmore, there flows a stream of Saxon gore,
And great is Rory Óg O'More at sending loons to Hades.
White is sick and Grey has fled, now for Black Fitzwilliam's head,
We'll send it over dripping red, to Liza and her ladies.

50

The Rising of the Moon

This song relates to the 1798 Rebellion. The air is 'The Wearing of the Green', and the lyrics were written by J.K. Casey (1846-1870), a Fenian from Mullingar.

Arrangement copyright Waltons Publications Ltd.

'Oh then tell me Sean O' Far-rell tell me why you hur-ry so,' 'Hush-a bhuach-aill hush and lis-ten,' and his cheeks were all a-glow, 'I bear or-ders from the cap-tain: Get you read-y quick and soon, For the pikes must be to-get-her at the ri-sing of the moon.' 'At the ri-sing of the moon,— at the ri-sing of the moon, For the pikes must be to-get-her at the ri-sing of the moon.'

'Oh, then tell me Sean O'Farrell, where the gath'ring is to be?'
'In the old spot by the river, right well known to you and me.
One word more, for signal token, whistle up the marching tune,
With your pike upon your shoulder at the rising of the moon.'
Chorus:–

Out from many a mud-wall cabin eyes were watching through that night,
Many a manly heart was throbbing for the blessed warning light.
Murmurs passed along the valleys, like the banshee's lonely croon,
And a thousand blades were flashing at the rising of the moon.
Chorus:–

There beside the singing river, that dark mass of men were seen,
Far above the shining weapons, hung their own beloved green.
'Death to every foe and traitor, forward, strike the marching tune,
And hurrah, my boys, for freedom, 'tis the rising of the moon!'
Chorus:–

Well they fought for poor old Ireland, and full bitter was their fate,
Oh! what glorious pride and sorrow fills the name of ninety-eight.
Yet, thank God, e'en still are beating, hearts in manhood's burning noon,
Who would follow in the footsteps at the rising of the moon!
Chorus:–

Mill Street, Monaghan

The Last Rose of Summer

Thomas Moore (1779-1852) wrote this song and set it to the air 'The Young Man's Dream'.

Arrangement copyright Waltons Publications Ltd.

'Tis the last rose of— sum-mer left— bloom-ing— a - lone. All her
love - ly com - pan - ions are— fa - ded— and—
gone. No— flow'r of— her— kind - red, no— rose - bud— is—
ni - gh, To re - flect back her— blu- shes, or to give sigh— for— sigh.

I'll not leave thee, thou lone one, to pine on the stem,
Since the lovely are sleeping, go sleep thou with them.
Thus kindly I scatter thy leaves o'er the bed,
Where thy mates of the garden lie scentless and dead.

So soon may I follow, when friendships decay,
And from love's shining circle the gems drop away.
When true hearts lie withered and fond ones are flown,
Oh! who would inhabit this bleak world alone?

The Threshing Engine

53

Master McGrath

This song tells the story of Lord Lurgan's greyhound, which won the Waterloo Cup in 1868, '69 and '71.
The dog died of pneumonia during Christmas of 1871. There are two monuments to him in Co. Waterford.

Arrangement copyright Waltons Publications Ltd.

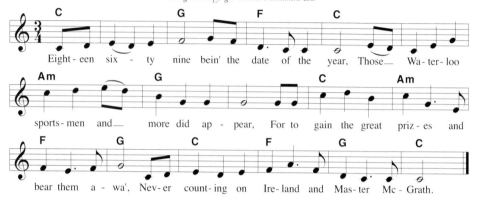

Eight-een six - ty nine bein' the date of the year, Those__ Wa-ter-loo
sports-men and__ more did ap - pear, For to gain the great priz-es and
bear them a - wa', Nev-er count-ing on Ire-land and Mas-ter Mc-Grath.

On the twelfth of November, that day of renown,
McGrath and his keeper they left Lurgan town.
A gale in the channel, it soon drove them o'er,
On the thirteenth they landed on England's fair shore.

Oh well, when they arrived in big London Town,
Those great English 'Sportsmen', they all gathered round.
And one of those gentlemen standing nearby
Said, 'Is that the great dog you call Master McGrath?'

Oh well, one of those gentlemen standing around
Says, 'I don't care a damn for your Irish greyhound.'
And another, he sneered with a scornful 'Ha! Ha!
We'll soon humble the pride of your Master McGrath.'

Then Lord Lurgan came forward and said, 'Gentlemen,
If there's any amongst you has money to spend,
For your grand English nobles I don't care a straw,
Here's five thousand to one upon Master McGrath.'

Oh McGrath he looked up and he wagged his old tail,
Informing his lordship, 'Sure I know what you mane.
Don't fear noble Brownlow, don't fear them agrá,
We'll soon tarnish their laurels,' says Master McGrath.

Oh well Rose stood uncovered, the great English pride,
Her master and keeper were close by her side.
They let them away and the crowd cried 'Hurrah'
For the pride of all England, and Master McGrath.

Oh well Rose and the Master, they both ran along.
'I wonder,' says Rose, 'what took you from your home.
You should have stayed there in your Irish domain,
And not come to gain laurels on Albion's plain.'

'Well, I know,' says the Master, 'we have wild heather bogs,
But, bedad, in old Ireland there's good men and dogs.
Lead on, bold Britannia, give none of your jaw,
Stuff that up your nostrils,' says Master McGrath.

Well the hare she led on just as swift as the wind,
He was sometimes before her and sometimes behind.
He jumped on her back and held up his ould paw.
'Long live the Republic,' says Master McGrath.

Harvesting

The Butcher Boy

This is a simple ballad of English origin. It tells the story of
love lost, leading to the final suicide of the heroine.

Arrangement copyright Waltons Publications Ltd.

In Moore— Street——— where I did dwell,—— A but-cher boy—
—— I loved right well.—— He cour-ted me—— my life a-way,—
—— And now with me—— he— will not stay.——

I wish my baby it was born, and smiling on his daddy's knee,
And my poor body to be dead and gone with the long green grass growing over me.

He went upstairs, the door he broke, he found her hanging by a rope.
He took a knife and cut her down, and in her pocket these words he found:

'Go dig my grave both wide and deep, put a marble stone at my head and feet,
And in the middle a turtle dove, to show the world that I died for love.'

Old Market Lane, Killarney, Co. Kerry

Alice Benbolt

Traditional

Arrangement copyright Waltons Publications Ltd.

Do you re - mem- ber sweet Al- ice, Ben- bolt? sweet Al- ice___ with hair___ of brown? Who wept with de - light___ when you gave her___ a smile___ And trem- bled___ to tears___ at your frown.___ In the old church - yard in the val- ley Ben - bolt, In a cor- ner obs - cure and___ a - lone, They have laid___ a piece of gra- nite___ so grey and sweet Al- ice___ lies un- der___ the stone.___ They have laid___ a piece___ of gra- nite___ so grey and sweet Al - ice___ lies un - der___ the stone.___

Do you remember the school Benbolt
And the masters so kind and true?
And that little nook by the babbling brook,
Where we gathered sweet flowers as they grew?
And all of the friends that were sweethearts then,
There's none left there but you and I.
And all of the friends that were sweethearts then,
There's none left there but you and I.
And all of the friends that were sweethearts then,
There's none left there but you and I.

57

Courtin' in the Kitchen

Traditional

Arrangement copyright Waltons Publications Ltd.

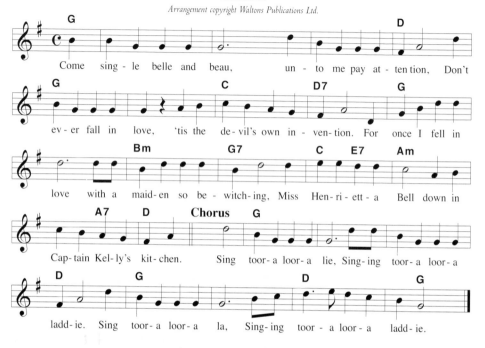

At the age of seventeen I was 'prenticed to a grocer,
Not far from Stephen's Green, where Miss Henri' used to go sir.
Her manners were so fine, she set me heart a-twitchin',
When she invited me to a hooley in the kitchen.

Sunday bein' the day we were to have the flare-up,
I dressed myself quite gay and I frizzed and oiled me hair up.
The Captain had no wife and he'd gone off a-fishin',
So, we kicked up high-life below stairs in the kitchen.

Just as the clock struck six, we sat down to the table,
She handed tea and cakes and I ate what I was able.
I had cakes with punch and tay, till me side had got a stitch in,
And the time passed quick away with our courtin' in the kitchen.

With me arms around her waist, she slyly hinted marriage,
When to the door in dreadful haste came Captain Kelly's carriage.
Her looks told me full well, and they were not bewitchin',
That she wished I'd get to hell, or somewhere from the kitchen.

She flew up off my knees, full five feet up or higher,
And over head and heels, threw me slap into the fire.
My new Repealer's coat that I bought from Mr. Mitchel,
With a thirty-shilling note went to blazes in the kitchen.

I grieved to see me duds all besmeared with smoke and ashes,
When a tub of dirty suds right in me face she dashes.
As I lay on the floor, the water she kept pitchin',
Till a footman broke the door and came chargin' in the kitchen.

When the Captain came downstairs, tho' he seen me situation,
Despite all me prayers I was marched off to the station.
For me they'd take no bail, tho' to get home I was itchin',
And I had to tell the tale of how I came into the kitchen.

I said she did invite me, but she gave a flat denial,
For assault she did indict me, and I was sent for trial.
She swore I robbed the house in spite of all her schreechin',
And I got six months hard for me courtin' in the kitchen.

The Shillelagh Seller

The Wild Colonial Boy

This 19th century ballad tells the story of Jack Donoghue, a native of Castlemaine, Co. Kerry.
He became a bush ranger in Australia and was killed by the mounted police.

Arrangement copyright Waltons Publications Ltd.

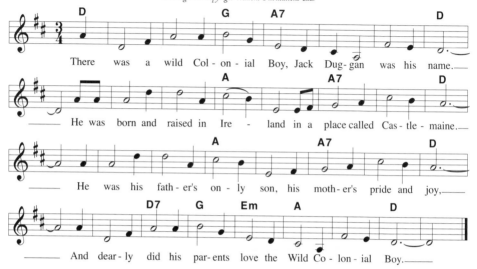

There was a wild Col - on - ial Boy, Jack Dug - gan was his name.—

He was born and raised in Ire - land in a place called Cas - tle - maine.—

He was his fath - er's on - ly son, his moth - er's pride and joy,—

And dear - ly did his par - ents love the Wild Co - lon - ial Boy.—

At the early age of sixteen years he left his native home,
And to Australia's sunny land, he was inclined to roam.
He robbed the rich and he helped the poor, he stabbed James MacEvoy.
A terror to Australia was the Wild Colonial Boy.

One morning on the prairie, wild Jack Duggan rode along,
While listening to the mocking bird, singing a cheerful song.
Out jumped three troopers, fierce and grim, Kelly, Davis and Fitzroy.
They all set out to capture him, the Wild Colonial Boy.

'Surrender now, Jack Duggan, you can see there's three to one,
Surrender in the Queen's name, sir, you are a plundering son.'
Jack drew two pistols from his side, and glared upon Fitzroy.
'I'll fight but not surrender,' cried the Wild Colonial Boy.

He fired a shot at Kelly, which brought him to the ground,
He fired point blank at Davis, too, who fell dead at the sound.
But a bullet pierced his brave young heart from the pistol of Fitzroy,
And that was how they captured him, the Wild Colonial Boy.

The Bard of Armagh

This song was probably written in the mid-19th century. The air is slow and
sad and was also used in America for 'The Streets of Laredo'.
Arrangement copyright Waltons Publications Ltd.

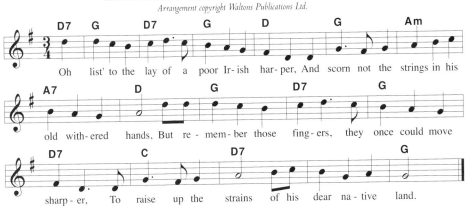

Oh list' to the lay of a poor Ir- ish har- per, And scorn not the strings in his
old with- ered hands, But re - mem- ber those fing- ers, they once could move
sharp - er, To raise up the strains of his dear na - tive land.

It was long before the shamrock, dear Isle's lovely emblem,
Was crushed in its beauty by the Saxon's lion paw,
And all the pretty colleens around me would gather,
Called me their bold Phelim Brady, the Bard of Armagh.

How I love to muse on the days of my boyhood,
Though four score and three years have fled by since then.
Still it gives sweet reflection, as every young joys should,
For the merry-hearted boys make the best of old men.

At a fair or a wake I would twist my shillelagh,
And trip through a dance with my brogues tied with straw.
There all the pretty maidens around me would gather,
Called me their bold Phelim Brady, the Bard of Armagh.

In truth I have wandered this wide world over,
Yet Ireland's my home and a dwelling for me.
And, oh, let the turf that my old bones shall cover
Be cut from the land that is trod by the free.

And when Sergeant Death in his cold arms doth embrace me,
And lulls me to sleep with old 'Erin-go-Bragh',
By the side of my Kathleen, my dear pride, oh, place me,
Then forget Phelim Brady, the Bard of Armagh.

Lanigan's Ball

This song is said to have originated in Athy, Co. Kildare around 1860.
Arrangement copyright Waltons Publications Ltd.

I stepped out, I stepped in again, I stepped in again, I stepped out again,
I stepped out and I stepped in again, learning to dance for Lanigan's Ball.

Myself to be sure got free invitations, for all the nice girls and boys I might ask,
And just in a minute both friends and relations were dancing as merry as bees 'round a cask.
There was lashings of punch and wine for the ladies, potatoes and cakes, there was bacon and tea,
There were Nolans, Dolans, O'Gradys, courting the girls and dancing away.

They were doing all kinds of nonsensical polkas, all 'round the room in a whirligig,
But Julia and I soon banished their nonsense, and tipped them a twist of a real Irish jig.
Oh, how that girl got mad on me and danced till you'd think the ceilings would fall,
For I spent three weeks at Brook's Academy, learning to dance for Lanigan's Ball.
Chorus:- and add (for this verse only)
I stepped out, I stepped in again, I stepped in again, I stepped out again,
I stepped out, I stepped in again, learning to dance for Lanigan's Ball.

The boys were as merry, the girls all hearty, dancing away in couples and groups,
Till an accident happened, young Terence Macarthy, he put his right foot through Miss Finerty's hoops.
The creature she fainted and cried 'Meelia murther', called for her brothers and gathered them all.
Carmody swore that he'd go no further, till he'd have satisfaction at Lanigan's Ball.

In the midst of the row Miss Kerrigan fainted, her cheeks at the same time as red as a rose,
Some of the boys decreed she was painted, she took a small drop too much, I suppose.
Her sweetheart Ned Morgan, so powerful and able, when he saw his fair colleen stretched by the wall,
He tore the left leg from under the table and smashed all the dishes at Lanigan's Ball.
Chorus:-

Boys, oh boys, 'tis then there was ructions, myself got a kick from big Phelim McHugh,
But soon I replied to his kind introduction, and kicked up a terrible hullabaloo.
Ould Casey, the piper, was near being strangled, they squeezed up his pipes, bellows, chanters and all,
The girls in their ribbons, they all got entangled, and that put an end to Lanigan's Ball.
Chorus:-

The West's Awake

This song was written by Thomas Davis (1814-1845), set to the air of 'The Brink of the White Rock'.
Arrangement copyright Waltons Publications Ltd.

That chainless wave and lovely land, Freedom and Nationhood demand.
Be sure the great God never planned for slumb'ring slaves a home so grand.
And long a brave and haughty race, honoured and sentinelled the place,
Sing, Oh! not even their sons' disgrace can quite destroy their glory's trace.

For often in O'Connor's van, to triumph dashed each Connaught clan.
And fleet as deer the Normans ran, thro' Curlieu's Pass and Ardrahan.
And later times saw deeds as brave, and glory guards Clanricarde's grave.
Sing, Oh! they died their land to save, at Aughrim's slopes and Shannon's wave.

And if, when all a vigil keep, the west's asleep, the west's asleep.
Alas and well may Erin weep, that Connaught lies in slumber deep.
But hark, a voice like thunder spake, the west's awake, the west's awake!
Sing, Oh hurrah! let England quake, we'll watch till death for Erin's sake.